A Trip Around Town

Learning to Add Three One-Digit Numbers

Amanda Boyd

Math for the REAL World™

Rosen Classroom Books & Materials
New York

My sister and I walk around town
every day.

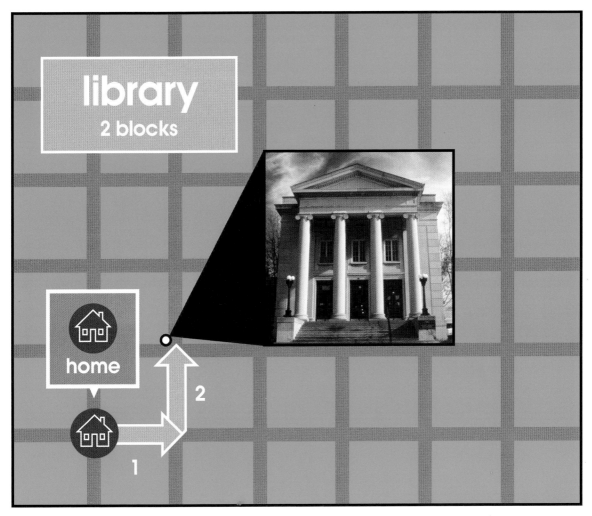

Yesterday we walked 2 blocks from home to the library.

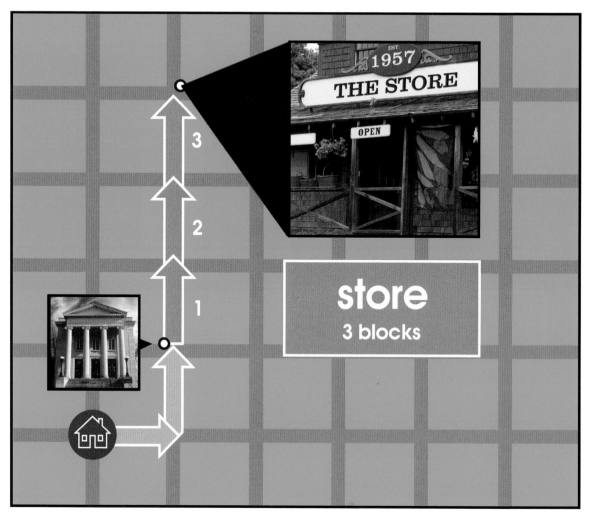

Then we walked 3 blocks from the library to the store.

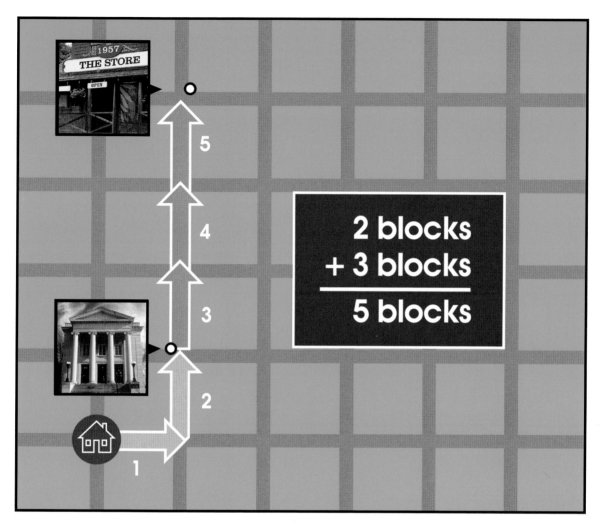

1957
THE STORE
OPEN

5
4
3
2
1

2 blocks
+ 3 blocks
5 blocks

How many blocks did we walk altogether?

We walked 5 blocks altogether.

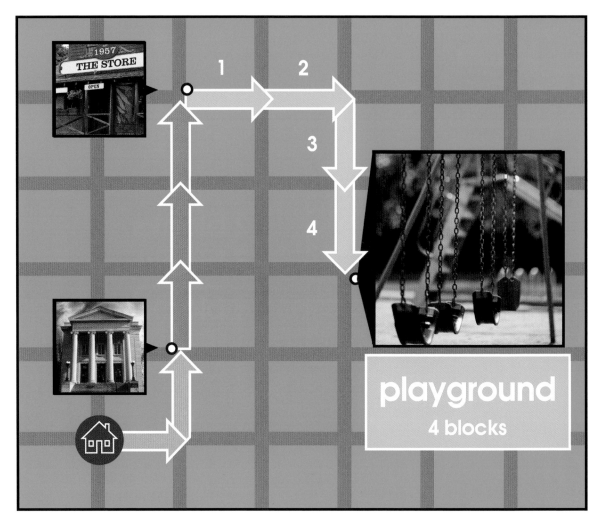

We left the store and walked 4 blocks to the playground.

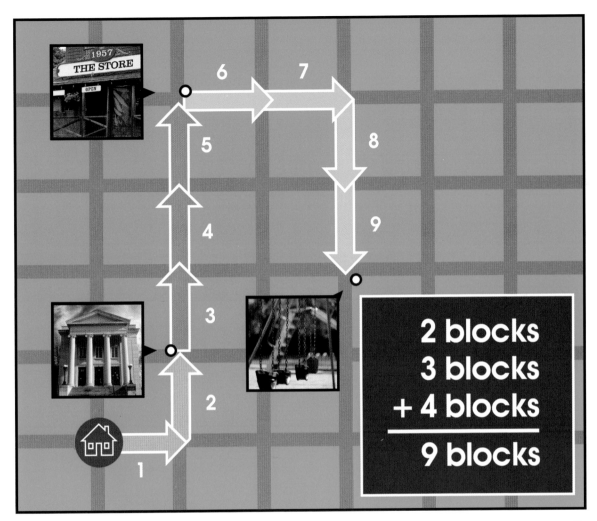

1957
THE STORE
OPEN

6   7

5   8

4   9

3

2

1

2 blocks
3 blocks
+ 4 blocks
_____
9 blocks

How many blocks did we walk altogether?

We walked 9 blocks altogether.

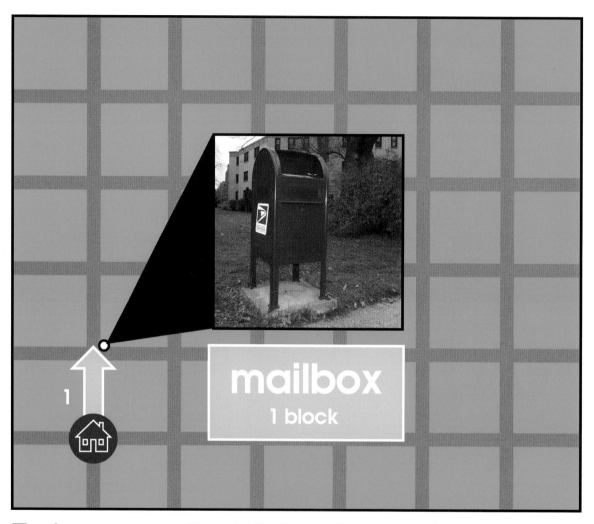

Today we walked 1 block from home to the mailbox.

Read all the books in this set!

MaryRuth BOOKS

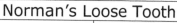

Norman's Loose Tooth
Level 9
Words 65

SongLake Books

ISBN 978-1-62544-162-1

90000>

9 781625 441621

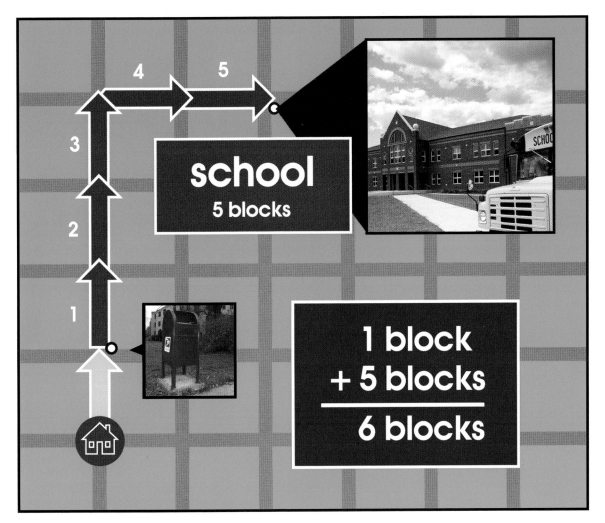

Then we walked 5 blocks from the mailbox to school. We walked 6 blocks altogether.

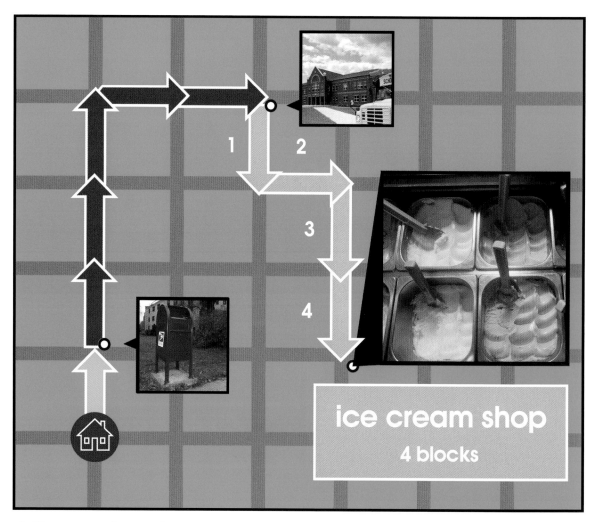

After school we walked 4 blocks to the ice cream shop.

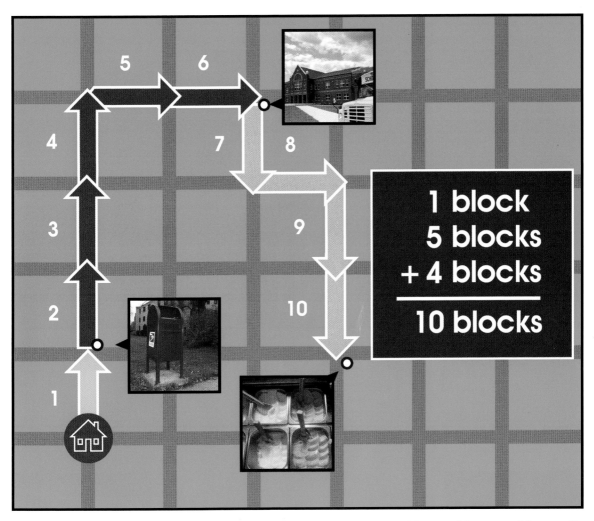

How many blocks did we walk altogether?

We walked 10 blocks altogether!

Words to Know

ice cream

library

mailbox

playground

school

store